PUNK WITH DULCIMER

PUNK WITH DULCIMER
ANNA CROWE

PETERLOO POETS

First published in 2006
by Peterloo Poets
The Old Chapel, Sand Lane, Calstock,
Cornwall PL18 9QX, U.K.

**A catalogue record for this book is available
from the British Library**

ISBN   1-904324-26-6

Printed in Great Britain by
Antony Rowe Ltd, Chippenham, Wilts.

ACKNOWLEDGEMENTS

Acknowledgements are due to the editors of the
following publications: *Island, The John Muir Trust
Journal, The London Magazine, New Writing Scotland,
Oxford Magazine, PN Review, Poetry Scotland, The Red
Wheelbarrow, Smiths Knoll, Sou'wester* (South Illinois
University), *Stand,* and *Tayside and Fife Archaeological
Journal.* In addition, some of the poems in *Punk with
Dulcimer* have been anthologised in *Edinburgh, An
Intimate City* (ed. Bashabi Fraser and Elaine Greig,
Edinburgh 2000), in *Scottish Poems* (ed. John Rice,
Macmillan 2001), and in the Tenth Anniversary Shore
Poets anthology, *Such Strange Joy* (ed. Allan Crosbie,
Iynx Publishing 2001). Some of these poems have
appeared in *A Secret History of Rhubarb*, a pamphlet of
poems published by Mariscat Press, 2004. 'Sufficient
Unto the Day' was a runner-up in the 1999 Peterloo
Open Poetry Competition.

"The heart is for saving what it can."
Laurence Sterne, *A Sentimental Journey*

For, don't you mark? we're made so that we love
First when we see them painted, things we have passed
Perhaps a hundred times, nor cared to see;
And so they are better, painted — better to us,
Which is the same thing. Art was given for that;
Robert Browning, *Fra Lippo Lippi*

CONTENTS

11 A Tentsmuir Flora
13 The Wemyss School of Needlework
    1. Patterns
    2. Pit-Head
    3. Pictures
17 Close
18 Maid's Room
19 The Italian Chapel, Orkney
20 Tibetan Prayer-Roll
22 The Extraction
24 Coming to Light
25 A Grand View of the Bay
27 Punk with Dulcimer
29 Out of the Dark-Room
31 Leavings
32 A Calendar of Hares
34 Nightjar
35 Deconstructing Winter
36 Persephone at the Burrell
37 The Map Maker
38 Sloes
39 Birdsong
40 Bog-bean at Red Myres Loch
41 From the Electricity Sub-Station
42 October Song
43 Interior
44 St Modomnoc's Bees
45 The Love-Knot
47 Imagining the Library
49 The Window-Cleaners
50 Greek Vase and Sussex Lady
51 Gollop's
53 Violet
54 Fretwork
55 A Spell in the Screw-Dock
56 The Kites of Liquorice Village

57 Homing
59 Firths and Sounds
60 Revising the Blue Guide to Scotland
63 Mended Fence, Barra
65 Parable
66 The Great Tay Wave
68 Eve of Another War
70 Underfoot
72 The Shadow
74 Primula Auricula
75 Cat and Water
76 The French for 'bonfire'
77 Sufficient Unto the Day
78 The Palm Magnificat
80 The Pattern of Our Days
82 The Bee-Bole Wall
83 Wedding Songs
85 Sari
87 Lady Prospero
88 Thistledown
89 The Burning-Bush
90 Water-Wheel
91 In the Alfàbia Gardens
93 Moon Into Marmalade
94 Scops Owl

A Tentsmuir Flora

"Existing floras exhibit only one moment in the history of the earth's
vegetation." Sir William Turner Thiselton-Dyer: 'Plant Distribution',
Encyclopaedia Britannica

A moment that you might fathom, you'd think,
reciting names like *adderstongue* and *moonwort*,
coralroot and *yellow birdsnest*,
listed in Tentsmuir's resonant flora.
But then an owl at Morton Lochs disgorges
a pellet packed with fieldmouse fur
and tiny bones from a neighbouring parish,
and seeds that will grow into another moment.

And there are days when haar drifts in from the sea
and settles like drops of mercury on rhubarb leaves,
when you step out into the garden,
into the moment before; digging, you unearth
bits of clay pipe, the bowl inscribed with
Masonic symbols: a pair of compasses
like a Pictish V-rod; in shifting light
your fossil-heap a shellfish-midden.

Moments washed by Forth and Tay; Fife
a mesopotamia of silts and erosions;
a kingdom stretched between its firths
like a hide from the scriptorium at Balmyrnie,
barley-fields the colour of vellum.
Earth you may as well be fathomed in, you think,
instinctively at home, peninsular,
putting down roots almost by accident.

You heard a story about a plant that sprang up
when a ship from Tierra del Fuego sank
at the mouth of the Tay; how Patagonian fleeces
hung for weeks on Tentsmuir's barbed-wire.
Wind was combing the wool with weavers' fingers,
as you remembered the Huguenots who fled
here in an earlier wave; loosened seeds
of *Norwegian Lamb's Lettuce* taking root.

The Wemyss School of Needlework

1. Patterns

The castle has turned its back,
closed on itself, a cold
stone bud with roots in coal.

In the lodge, miners' daughters
wore scalloped aprons, sleeve-protectors.
Hands were scrubbed, *hands*
at all times were to be clean.
They shook cloth on to trestles,
laying swathes of paper, stamped
with pomegranates, thistles;
hearing,
as fingers smoothed out creases,
the faintest whisper of
fleur-de-lys; a dead
queen's handwork
they pricked with holes.

Tissue was perforated;
charcoal, sifted through,
tracing the branching forms
of *bronchii* and *alveoli*.
Coal-dust stole their fathers' breath;
emphysema worked its mossy pattern.

Daylight comes through a faint
suggestion of wires —
a dressmaker's dummy from which
fully two thousand smocks took flight.
Propped in incongruous boots
it leans like a second lattice
against the dusty window.
As though the last one to be dressed
had left her bones behind,

the gathered flesh fallen like silk.
Wires fastened on air, it hangs
like a cage awash with
everything that has vanished;
listing, abandoned, into the light.

The Wemyss School of Needlework was founded by Miss Dorothy Wemyss in
1877, to teach all aspects of embroidery to the daughters of miners in pits
owned by the Wemyss family.

2. Pit-Head

Trespass here, your feet will wake the cinders.
Dismal brickwork, stagnant water, scabs
of moss. The winding-gear bleakly heraldic,
the cable hanging slackly from its wheel —
machinery like a gigantic, rusted Singer
someone has dumped. They keep a guard
to bawl out trespassers. He springs from his hut
rejoicing in an entry for his log.
The Michael broods on thirty-odd years of silence —
a mouth that gulped down men and spewed up coal.
Lives that hung by a thread as the cage dipped
went swinging like canaries into the dark.

> Their flesh how easily mangled.
> Their bones how casually crushed
> by slusher or runaway drum.
> Rockfalls buried them forever.
> Firedamp blew them to kingdom come.
> The *Lady Victoria* stamped her foot.
> And *Lady Emma* thumped her cane.
> But *Michael*, the Captain, lit them like candles
> and bellowed until he was dumb.

Men unfolded rock and worked it like cloth.
Bodies, thin as lutestring, sea-plucked, needled
into narrow holes. Beads of jet clung
to stump-work, crewel-work, drawn-thread-work.
The tented dark shook out taffeta gleams
from wet rock, the black seam leading them
ever further from shore, until the fabric tore
and the mine blew to a roaring furnace.

Later, oil-rigs dandered up the Forth
and anchored. There's one there yet.
At night it's a brand-new constellation,
but during the day you hardly see it. Graffito
like a Pictish symbol, or initials on a giro.

The *Victoria, Lady Emma* and the *Michael* are all names of pits in the Wemyss
area, named for members of the Wemyss family. The name *Wemyss* comes
from *uamh,* the Gaelic for *cave*.

3. Pictures

Behind the street, the sea has broached its wall,
and miners' homes are derelict, their frontage
now a film-set; *trompe-l'oeil* doorways painted
ajar; windows with two-dimensional cats
or flower-pots. Only the hotel is real.

Here in the Needlework School, damp and moss
embroider cracks like monograms on trousseaux.
Names have gone to holes, whole dynasties
unravelled in a fraying of seams. Ghost-
like, this daughter of Wemyss, who stares from her
      portrait

over the heaped-up silk, bargello, quilting:
bad luck has cracked the glass, so that it might
indeed be a mirror, the way the window's caught
and fractured; as though exemplifying faulting
or the way light bends as it enters water.

Did she, a child awake at night, hear
her father's miners tapping beneath the roots
of the house? The sound would haunt her, change her —
the way a fault will split a wall from foot
to crown when something deep-down shifts.

Rock is still on the move, rumbling inwards
to stop and seal-up pits and holes. Wemyss
is an eye, closing. One by one, the caves
fold up their pictures, and Pictish beasts, birds,
fish, even the odd ship, swim into the dark.

Close

They are still here, the walled-up dead.
Their stifled cries, a tightness in the chest;
blood pounding in our ears,
their fists on doors.

This slum is under the street.
Above us, twelve or thirteen floors
rise like Babel into Edinburgh's night:
chandeliers, mirrors, portraits,
Scotland's history, sins of the fathers.

When they unblocked the close,
moist, damp air blew in,
and in the butcher's shop
faded stains in the plaster
freshened and bloomed.

Those who came on Egypt's royal dead
uncorked a stoppered air,
catching a breath of spikenard or myrrh
before it sighed and was gone.

Stumbling over cobbles, our feet disturb
a whiff of byre — cow-dung
and sweetly, faintly, hay;
round the next corner,
brief, fragrant, unmistakable,
baking bread.

Mary King's Close lies beneath the City Chambers in Edinburgh. In the 17th
century, the authorities ordered it to be bricked-up — along with its inhabitants
— during an outbreak of plague.

Maid's Room

(for Leisha)

The combed ceiling hoards up whispers, sighs,
a crackle of anger, a creak of stays.
Stripping paper under the baking slates
you eavesdrop on the previous folk — lives
of careful garlands, furrows dull and straight —
stiff generations falling down in sheaves.

But when your scraper calls up heartbeats, dust
is suddenly tenanted, the room opening
like a kiss: the tongue-and-groove of lost
Scots pine, and in the air the sweat of resin.
And you know she is close enough to touch — skin
burnished like wood, her hair in knots; just
wakened and still in her shift, in a haze of daisies
you'll never uproot, rub out, or will away.

The Italian Chapel, Orkney

Even the Romanesque façade —
Santa Croce in eight-foot driftwood —
can't quite prepare us for this shift
of light, from cold Orcadian
to golden Tuscan radiance.

Painted bricks in the Nissen's vault
lodge in the throat like grief, and fake
marble takes us in — as walls
are meant to — out of the cold. Northern
winters taught them perfect brushwork.

On islands bare of trees, their calendar's
scored-out days stretched, perhaps,
to a memory of cypresses.
A neutral ocean tossed up scraps
of wood and metal they could use.

At first they stretched barbed wire across
the sanctuary, where mother and child
wait as they've always done,
and the colour of Mary's dress
is the sea that lies between.

I want to think they painted grief
away for a space, laying such shadows
on plaster-board that all their patterns
sprang to life, ran free; each linked relief
reaching from Lamb Holm to Italy.

The Italian Chapel was built from two Nissen huts by Italian PoWs at
Camp 60, Lamb Holm, Orkney, in 1942-3, and decorated by Domenico
Chiochetti and others.

Tibetan prayer-roll

(for Christopher)

"when the wind is southerly, I know a hawk from a handsaw."
Shakespeare, *Hamlet*

Your grandfather brought it back
from India where he spent the war
battling against his stammer
while teaching the troops to read,
and to read Shakespeare.

The prayer-roll has come down to us
wrapped in a scrap of soft, ragged cloth
the colour of reddish earth, woven
heaven knows how, the weave and cross-
weave pulling every which way;
pieced together like small brown fields,
terraced patches that hug the skirts of mountains
and are just big enough to sustain
a crop of millet, or two goats,
or a single apple-tree.

The paper is wrinkled, soft,
the colour of old stamp-hinges.
We can't unroll it completely —
perhaps the glue that joins its inner strips
spread when rain or snow seeped in.
Of the six lines of writing, wood-block-
printed, that pack its length,
five repeat the same prayer
in silent unison, in a language
I cannot read, a script that teems with birds:
here's a character stalks the line like a gull
behind the plough, another stooping
pelican-like above her young, or poised
like a bony heron in a burn; or a hawk,

happier riding a southerly wind, fluent
and lucid as this was once, birling
high above fields and villages, in a silence
greater than all the sounds of war.

The Extraction

After the screams as saws bit into steel,
and crump as girders fell;
after the bucketing sobs of JCBs
and crackle of fires,
silence falls like an armistice.

Huge space fills the window — sky appears,
and other gardens, slates and chimneys,
gabled lives. A gap our eyes return to
again, the way the tongue will probe
the socket left by a tooth.

But there's a chunk of oral history
the team down on their hands and knees,
scraping and brushing their tagged trenches,
will find no evidence for. The shed once housed
Hermann Göring's bullet-proof limo.

While hectoring me mildly on broad beans,
William Duncan, my dentist, dropped
this information into my open mouth.
He filled or pulled the teeth
of German POWs after the war,

and one was Göring's driver,
Werner Pfusch, a Munich window-cleaner,
a man on the outside, looking in. And good
at his job, because that car would need a hell
of a lot of cleaning. Göring would want to see

his face in it; want to be seen, and see
all round, as in the cockpit
of his Messerschmitt, re-living
that last dog-fight over Flanders... a small
cloud spoils his vision, an oily smear

on the inside of the glass. No matter
how much Göring raged or Werner rubbed,
it always reappeared. It smelt
like the filthy smoke that hung around that camp
he'd had to drive to. Even now, spreading

muck on fields in Angus, he can taste it.
He spits into an icy furrow,
wiping his mouth on his sleeve.
Scheiss! That tooth was stabbing again.
This time he hoped they'd pull it out.

Coming to Light

Ten years after the end of the war,
and things were beginning to surface:
the eagle-headed bottle-stopper,

made of glass, that came to light
between the floor-boards in the attic.
German officers had lived here

in *'Sous les Tilleuls'*, the house they called
'Unter den Linden'; but I remember
the day you drove an old woman away,

bawling her out for picking lime-flowers
from the trees outside our gate; the iron
clang as it slammed, the garden

shrinking into darkness. Yet maybe
that was just a trick of the light,
my dazzling element that carved

everything into black and white.
Slowly our horizons grew, and I saw
how the sun sank into the great red arms

of the cedar at the road's end
like the *pietà* on the wall at school;
how the smell of roasting coffee — blown

from the *torréfaction*, two streets away —
came with the promise of rain; finding,
when I climbed the spiral stair to the tower

and emerged into the sun,
that I was tall enough, suddenly,
to see a rim of light that could only be the sea.

A Grand View of the Bay

(i.m. Jessie Ireland)

I'm thinking how your eyes would sparkle
to see this plastic grass, lining your grave —
an emerald baize beloved of Lammas markets,
harvest-festivals, breezy greengrocers.
The way it hides raw earth with cheerful cladding,
like you, down on your hands and knees to coax
another sullen gleam out of the lino:
Marine Place, after the hurricane.
The Sea Box Co.'s two damp rooms
where overnight your shoes would bloom with mould.

From time to time, your life
shot into headlines from the *Sunday Post*:
— BUDGIE SAVED HER LIFE IN HURRICANE
TERROR —
— BEE-STING KEEPS FATHER HOME AS SHIP GOES
DOWN —
— WOMAN GIVES GOLDFISH KISS OF LIFE —
Canvassed at seventy on the American bombing
of North Vietnam, you sided with Hanoi,
thumping the table, making the doilies tremble.
Bombing folk oot o' their hooses? No me!
Ah wis bombed oot in the gales!
Ah ken whit like it is tae loss yer hame.

You lost your *grand view of the bay* —
Tentsmuir's horizons; Arbroath sparkling at night
like diamonds on a ring, impossibly far.
Fretting you'd up and marry, your father would stand,
you said, at the top of the close, peering the length
of North Street, shading his eyes against disaster.
Ah niver had a jo. I heard a kind of
wondering grief, tempered by pride.

The other *Jockies* & *Joeys*, your *Bobbies* & *Billies*,
and the one who turned out to be *Billiamina*,
laying one small cold egg, are long since
tucked up under the turf.
And they're burying you with Snowy the doll
who came with some shortbread, silently, one Christmas.
The shadow of St Rule's
leans out across your grave:
your father still speiring after you,
and you just gone for messages
Or off to meet some fancy fella.

Punk with Dulcimer

He stood at the end of the carriage.
A black-clad giant, fearsome
in fringed and studded leather, ginger mohican.
Then sat down in the seat beside me.

Soon — *Plants are amazing, so they are!*
The voice, rich Ulster. He looks up from his book,
eyes shining under the tawny crown.
— *If it weren't for plants,*
if it weren't for vascular bundles,
we'd not be walking upright.
He speaks in a creaking of leather,
a sound like branches in a pine-wood,
rubbing. And a multitude of studs,
from his ears to his bare, braceleted arms
and eloquent knuckle-dustered mittens,
sparkle and gleam like rain on thistles.

He is a green man speaking leaves.
Rainforest canopy fills the carriage
with rustled whispers; words
that make Linnaean music, space
for colobus, catleya, bell-bird
to peep from the fringes of speech.

For an hour he held sway, in language
as way above my head as, say, a sequoia.
Elusive as jaguar, and all gone.
All but those resonant, homely
vascular bundles. Oh, and the dulcimer.
He played a dulcimer in a folk-group,
was going, in fact, to play it in Newcastle
where he duly got off the train.

I think of how I had feared him,
of how we fear what we don't know.
And when I hear the whistles and drums
of marching Orangemen on the news,
I try to imagine the tune arranged for dulcimer
— hearing soft-struck strings;
seeing a black-clad figure,
tall as a cedar of Lebanon, and dancing.
Like David with his psaltery
before the Lord.

Out of the Dark-Room

(in memory of the photographer, Wyn Jones)

Some lost things I still grieve for.
A print of Antwerp Cathedral,
rolled-up and fallen years ago
behind the booming piano of my head,
goes on plucking twangs of regret.

Beneath that airy spire
I heard Allegri's *Miserere* sung —
a piece of Sistine property Mozart
strolled away with, leading it out
of Vatican gloom and into the light.

All of which brings me along the road
to Thomas Rodger's house. To learn
how he used his old photographic plates —
the first of their kind — to build himself
a greenhouse. Imagine it standing

like a piece of photosynthesis, as glass
breathed out Balmoral's crinolines
and Presbyterian sabbath gloom
and the burgh's darkest wynds and closes,
in favour of green leaves.

Picture the stiff Victorian whiskers
softening into tendrilled vines,
and whaleboned backs relaxed as jasmine.
Sun leaned in, and rubbed its fingers daily
on the glass, to get a better look

at peaches and pelargoniums,
baking plumbago into cherry-pie.
Was he blind, the man who ordered
its demolition? Picture the glum expressions
standing among the smithereens

as, here and there, a spectral eye
glared from the wreck of that museum.
If I shut mine, I see my print, hanging
high on a wall in clear light.
As high as the castor-oil plant

that is almost a tree. In Thomas Rodger's
garden against his house it thrives
without the benefit of glass.
Sun on the solid gloss of its leaves
dazzles. The wind plays it like harp.

Leavings

(for Simon Taylor)

"The plough still fetches stones from that patch there."
Noses over the wall, his pair of Clydesdales
nod, then snort and turn, a swirl of tails.
Kinnear's swallows graze the August air.

Stubble keeps whispering something as we pass.
Bishop and priests who would have walked this march
hover, their tongues wagging, helping us search
for *fons* and *alba rupis*. Their *magnus lapis* —

Muckle stane — is gone, the white crag doubtful.
The spring's been sealed where men would splash the
    sweat
of harvest from their faces. And yet our feet
leave the same imprimatur in the soil.

The Glack is curled between hills, cupping its hand
around our afternoon; nettles where five
then just two families of weavers lived.
Then the Kinnear shepherd. Folded ground.

Our fingers feel through moss to read the *K*
on boundary-stones. In gateways, warmer, clearer,
the scent of trampled matricaria;
and stubble-fires, now that they've baled the hay,

blowing in thin bronze drifts on Gallow Hill.
We see more clearly now we have climbed this far.
Far-off, and north, Cairngorm. Below, Kinnear.
A dark patch in one field that was the mill.

Kinnear, Kilmany parish, Fife, 31st August 1996

Latin terms from the Kinnear charter of 1260: *fons*, a spring;
alba rupis, white rock or crag; *Magnus lapis*, large stone or *muckle stane*

A Calendar of Hares

(for Valerie Gillies)

1. At the raw end of winter
the mountain is half snow, half
dun grass. Only when snow
moves does it become a hare.

2. If you can catch a hare
and look into its eye,
you will see the whole world.

3. That day in March
watching two hares boxing
at the field's edge, she felt
the child quicken.

4. It is certain Midas never saw a hare
or he would not have lusted after gold.

5. When the buzzard wheels
like a slow kite overhead
the hare pays out the string.

6. The man who tells you
he has thought of everything
has forgotten the hare.

7. The hare's form, warm yet empty.
Stumbling upon it, he felt his heart
lurch and race beneath his ribs.

8. Beset by fears, she became
the hare who hears
the mowers' voices growing louder.

9. Light as the moon's path over the sea,
the run of the hare over the land.

10. The birchwood a dapple
of fallen gold: a carved hare
lies in a Pictish hoard.

11. Waking to the cry of a hare
she ran and found the child sleeping.

12. November stiffens
into December: hare and grass
have grown a thick coat of frost.

Nightjar

(i.m. the sculptor, Keeble Smith)

You've slipped away, gone
to ground like your beloved adders
that hot afternoon, years ago now.
Although you knew their pathways,
where they came to drink,
all their favourite basking places,
not one did we happen upon;
the S-is-for-snake missing,
erased from the baking day.

Alice Holt, the summer of '88.
A log-jam of dead trees to the horizon,
a shock of scalped pines on the ridge.
We picked our way round sandy craters,
round snarls of roots nesting nowhere.
On every side the eye swam
dizzily into hurricane's thumbprints,
into whorled branches that mimicked
the stilled eddyings of huge air.

Back in the cottage, your adders
had glided into lime or chestnut
and lay like pools of themselves —
a spill of coils only the nightjar
could outshine: that perfect marriage
of grain and plumage; a deadleaf
tumult of burr-wood, those barrings
crowding like isobars; the forest
pivoting around the unwinking eye.

Deconstructing Winter

Every year you learn it the hard way:
a semiotics of cold that wind dins
into you until you have it by heart —
its ear-ache drone, its keyhole whine.

Frost you have at your fingertips.
Its rules are simple: a black frost means
weak birds invariably decline; whereas
hoar-frost favours the fairy-tale, rewards
humility with godmotherly largesse.
Take the back-garden, where dazzling marginalia
may suddenly appear on leaves, defy translation;
and the shed-window — all year a transparent Cinderella —
may suddenly publish a densely-worded work on rare
    ferns.

Meaning's encoded, too deep to dig for—
form coiled as tight as an ammonite,
the garden wall a library
on the hermeneutics of the snail.
Acknowledging a debt to Sterne, snow
offers the reader days of blank pages.

A shiver of robin-song, and it's March —
Still Janus-days when you stare into haar's drift
in search of a *but* or an *and*.
But it's when the blackbird in the viburnum sings
that you twig: icicles melting in that *pink-pink-pink*.

Persephone at the Burrell

The calm terracotta brow,
unseeing gaze and faintly smiling mouth —
all these proclaim the goddess. And yet
she is unmistakably
someone's daughter.

Implicit in that coiled crown of braids,
a mother's aching fingers,
making her beautiful
before sending her out to
God knows what rendez-vous.

From another room
my daughter catches my eye,
her smile travelling through case after
glass case of pots, cups, bowls, to eclipse
these gathered grave-goods.

The Map Maker

(i.m. Jen Downing)

At first it looks like disaster.
The wall split from top to bottom.   Your life
about to collapse in falling masonry.

The stairs float you upwards,
but even before one hand goes out to explore
the damage, the play of light tells you

one edge is roughly patterned,
and your fingers fit perfectly into flutings
that indicate the presence of cliffs.

Words swim up, like *cave* and *blow-hole*;
harbour in gothic script; and you know it's a map —
a chunk of east coast, maybe local.

North of the harbour,
beneath the wavy lines the sea is making,
you read *submerged settlement*;

in fact, it is possible to follow
the broken line of a wall into the water,
which is less cold than you thought.

Close up, two dotted lines of track
turn out to be footprints deeply carved in rock.
But after all, what is a path

but footprints; the tread of generations;
the latest erasing the ones before, making
a path for those who follow.

That's why it feels quite safe
to step into them and start walking; even though
the path leads straight out to sea.

Sloes

(on the death of a child)

have you seen a hedge at winter's end
go billowing down to a grey sea;
flowers that you mistake for cloud or a late frost?

this is the sloe, the black-
thorn, that blooms before the leaves unfurl
that wears no green in her bone-thin blossoming
but only thorns
grievous and long

she will not stay for us
her petals melt
like hailstones on the tongue

once fledged, her leaves
pierce your heart with their tender green
and in their midst the fruit ripens
blue-black, beautiful
gentled with bloom
like shadow on snow

with the first frosts
(the wild geese harking overhead
on their urgent journeys)
you gather them to steep in spirit,

marvelling, as the months pass,
how darkness clears to this true fire
how bitterness will distil such sweetness on the air

Birdsong

(for Ann and Bernard, in memory of Christopher, 1976- 2001)

Fledgling

As we turned into your drive I glimpsed the sparrow-
hawk's barred plumage where it sat among grasses
on the verge. It was in your garden later
that you remembered the afternoon it stooped
in a slight fluster of feathers to lift a young
thrush from off the lawn. And this was June
drenched in philadelphus, lovely, and ruined
for you, everything tasting of grief. And I wanted
a bird to open its throat and pour out pure
sound, wordless, and singing because it must.

Fountains Abbey

We searched but never found the Green Man
high in the arching tracery of the windows.
He had gone back to the woods, gone home: deep
in oak and birch, with thrush and wren he bides
his time. And from his mouth green branches grow,
and on the air his breath is a breeze blown
from the Skell, all elderflower and guelder-roses.

Homing

Slowing to take the bend at Low Cocklaw
before climbing into summer dusk
we heard a blackbird sing: no more than four
clear notes that fell like water drops
to still a world we had distressed with passing.

Bog Bean at Red Myres Loch

(i.m. Anne O'Donnell)

Menyanthes trifoliata — a flower
St Patrick might have plucked
from black bog-water,
holding aloft its three-in-one
leaf to exemplify the Trinity —
I first saw in your pond
at Falkland: a marrying
of the robust and delicate;
as tight, red buds relaxed,

released into a dazzle
of pink corollas so pale
as to be almost white,
with petals the guide describes
as *fimbriate* — though I prefer
the workaday *fringed* with its
faint suggestion of skin's
pallor tinged with Gerard's
'wash of slight Carnation'—

each spike held aloft
particular in its beauty,
it joins the flock hovering
above the lochan's surface: feet
in earth, rising through water,
faces upturned to the blue
that finds an answer — so thick
does bog-bean flourish here —
mid-lochan, in a quiet clearing.

From the Electricity Sub-Station

c. 1850 the Old Reading Room, Falkland

Then Thomas Drysdale laid aside his tools —
hammers that had tapped the names of the dead;
chisels, conversant with the skull and hour-
glass and the hard facts of numbers — to lift
a book and read aloud. A voice like Moses'
thundering out of Lomond; lightning-rod,
galvanising fellow-burghers with ballads,
with Covenanters' tales, whose severed hands
wrote their histories in the dust. As current
writings crackled into life, the room
turned transmission-chamber, fizzy with static,
the air smelling of smithy and tempered iron.
Nails were heard to buzz in the joists like bees.
The family of thirteen up the stair
drew sparks from one another's clothes, their hair
on end like wire, the dog beside himself;
the smallest child rolling a spangled ball
of cold St Elmo's fire about the floor.

While Thomas read, energy flowed like truth,
and lovers found their voice, declared their hearts;
the stammerer cleared his throat and smiled, then spoke,
and all things moved towards the light of day.
Pattullo's ancient ploughman, writing his best
lines across the in-field at Lathrisk,
heard the clang of a bell deep in the earth
and checked his team; and turning, saw a wall
of dressed stone haul itself free of the furrow,
and guessed those tales of Athernase's priory
might be true. Elsewhere, a hoard of silver
told on itself, ringing, high in the chimney;
and in the mason's house, his hammers chuckled
like jackdaws in their case; his chisels, each
in its oiled cerament, were heard to sing.

October Song

(for Douglas Dunn on his 60th birthday)

Why is it no surprise to learn October's
When your birthday falls? The fall of the leaf
And summer's silks suddenly turned to burrs

Compose Marvellian calendars of grief
You've made your own. Your lyric skies are pure
October blue, a tent to shelter waif

And witch, sad buskers, gaberlunzies. Grower
Of lilies, loving the sax's voice, the five
a.m. aubade the Moonzie sings, you outstare

Winter. Tuscan skies in Fife you give
Us, breaking our hearts with rainbows over the Tay;
An agate's bays; a shore on which to live

That's nowhere and yet everywhere. A day-
Light of the heart and mind; your open country.

Interior

Beach-glass, aquamarine;
the colour that clear shallows wear in the west,
at Back of Keppoch, say, or Arisaig.

Scoured by the back and forth of tides
this greeny-blue half neck of a medicine bottle
has coarsened; rub its tetchy frost

and it leaves a rasp of salt on your skin,
a sound like surf. But slip it on to your finger,
its silken glovework will seduce you —

the inner runnel hidden; the glimpsed
sheen of a mollusc's coiled interior;
the oiled machinery of the ear.

St Modomnoc's bees

(for Jess)

Below Kilnaughton the Singing Sands were hushed —
tide at the turn,
sea holding its breath.
But here, outside the small shell of the church,
air roared like a furnace
and we stood deafened and stunned, the afternoon
beating upon our ears like a bell.

And then you saw how the verge shimmered,
urgent with wings, and the more we stared,
the more it seemed that the ground crawled or flew.
Bees, bees in their thousands, burrowing-bees,
fervently coming and going through clover,
gathering pollen and nectar, provisioning cells:

a fierce continuum we stepped through, sharing
their summer's brief, these dogged husbandries.
Kilnaughton's stones were an open boat
we climbed down into, a coracle
of turf and grave-slabs, knapweed and tormentil.

As though we might put to sea with our dead
and sail across to Ireland, like that saint
whose bees refused to leave him — like these
whose noise out-sings the roar of cars
in Hackney streets, and will not let you go.

Islay, August 2004

The Love-Knot

Because I'm away from home — a firth, a sea,
an ocean between us — I thought I'd send you
the Shrine of St Patrick's Bell (it's in Dublin,
in the Museum — but so what? Not
for nothing do they call it the *Bell of the Will*).

I want you to see for yourself how weathered
and strong it is: the shape of a bell,
not rounded and smooth, but beaten bronze,
quadrangular, lumpy with imperfections:
there are gemstones missing — lost

like grand ideas in the rub of living —
or sold for food. Those that remain —
rock-crystal and garnets —
are set in cabochons so rough
they look like pools of rain, or drops of blood.

Donal O'Loughlin, King of Ireland,
had it made to enshrine the kind of bell
that hangs from a collar worn by the leading cow,
as the bellowing procession slowly climbs
and clangs its way to summer pasture:

a reliquary like the Book of Kells,
panelled in gold and intricate silver-gilt,
all sinewy variations on the love-knot:
thumb-prints, treble-clefs, ram's horns;
bestiaries of snipe, chimeras, serpents,

swimming elephants so joyfully, so
impossibly intertwined, there's no
beginning and no end; all roads,
flight-path and transhumance,
tugging us home. These gauzy puzzles

are the ones I'll see beneath me
from the plane: ring-roads and towns,
estates like webs of light; an interlace
of who we are; the unseen roofs
and silent coverings of love.

Imagining the Library

after Michelangelo's plan for the Laurentian Small Library

(i.m. Ferdy and Buffer Woodward)

Red-brown ink, rusted like blood:
this library within a library, walled and enclosed,
is worked like a blunt elbow
beautifully darned.

Designed to be *small* and *secret*,
to house the most precious books;
the image persists like knotwork,
a maze you might enter at dusk
led by the scent of box and clove-pinks,
calling the name of a cat you once had as a child.

Now that you're lost among quicksets
savour the word *pleasaunce* on your tongue,
following the names of plants down to their roots;
feeling for bistort and catnip,
houndstongue, lungwort, feverfew.

The body was where he started from.
Beside the plan in a small, clear hand
he gives the scale: a thumb-joint's length
to represent one *bracio.*
Picture him pacing, stretching out both his arms
to measure fathoms of air; imagining
for a curving wall's recess
that hollow above the collar-bone
where languid Adam's arm travels towards
a galvanic meeting of finger-tips.

But now, sit on the round stone bench, here
where no-one ever sat before;
and while you read
it will come to you in a murmur of leaves
that the library was never built
until this moment.

bracio (Italian, now *braccio*); an arm; yard, ell; flight of steps

The Window-Cleaners

(for Margaret)

arrive in a clatter of ladders —
men in boots, with cloths and buckets
and aprons, tools in pockets,
who have the look of mediaeval cathedral-builders;

who climb as though to the clerestory
up to our second-floor windows,
where they proceed to douse
the glass, erasing one month's history

of weather. These are the same who, sober-
suited, rang this Christmas
morning to bear witness
on our doorstep, pressing *The Watchtower*

into reluctant hands. Now, they scour
each pane as though it were
a soul, splashing water
with rough baptismal ardour.

Haloed in soap, close to the telegraph-wires'
dismal humming,
they'll greet the Second Coming
of the Lord. Till then, regular

as rain, they rise like messengers
from an unsullied Eden —
poised above frozen gardens,
grave men in woolly hats whom light transfigures.

Greek Vase and Sussex Lady

(in memory of Claire Crowe)

The sideboard stiff with scones and tea-bread,
at least three kinds of cake;
your table was a dazzling beach
where silver gleamed like fish.
You sat and poured Darjeeling from a blue
and gold pot; white-haired, still beautiful;
black velvet ribbon and cameo at your throat.

This is how I remember you, and yet —
roller-skating in nineteen hundred and seven,
the first girl in your road to ride a bike —
you were the one who plunged
into the Black Sea out of Sussex,
out of your family of Brethren, teetotal
to the bone; to surface with this drinking-
cup: two-handled *kantharos*; elegant
terracotta bossy with barnacles,
with wormy scribblings white as Downland chalk.

Some five years after your death,
we're celebrating the move to the new house,
broaching your last bottle of blackberry wine.
Twice the strength of conventional stuff,
more potent than any Hippocrene
that might have brimmed your Attic cup,
it's fairly laid us out among the tea-chests.
Sprawled in an orgy of bubble-wrap
with piled-up crockery and dusty books,
it is as much as we can do
to raise our helpless glasses and salute you —
Lady of Eastbourne galloping off
on a horse of Sussex chalk;
sea-nymph roller-skating out of sight.

Gollop's

(for Rosy)

Gollop was our grandmother's butcher.
Saying his name out loud, you swallowed
a lump of gristle whole. Even the thought
of going to Gollop's made us gulp,
made my little green-eyed sister's eyes
grow rounder, greener. Swags of rabbits
dangled at the door in furry curtains;
their eyes milky, blood congealed
around their mouths like blackcurrant-jelly.
You'd to run a gauntlet of paws.

Inside, that smell of blood and sawdust
still in my nostrils. Noises. The thump
as a cleaver fell; flinchings, aftershocks
as sinews parted, bone splintered.
The wet rasp of a saw. My eyes
were level with the chopping bench.
Its yellow wood dipped in the middle
like the bed I shared with Rosy.
Sometimes a trapdoor in the floor
was folded back. Through clouds of frost
our eyes made out wooden steps, then
huge shapes shawled in ice — the cold-store.

Into which the butcher fell,
once, bloody apron and all.
When my grandparents went to see
Don Juan, and told us how it ended
— *Like Mr Gollop!* I whispered.
Mr Gollop only broke his leg, but
> *Crash! Bang! Wallop!*
> *Went Mr Gollop!*
we chanted from our sagging bed,
giggles celebrating his downfall,
cancelling his nasty shop.
As the Co-op did a few years later
when it opened on the High Street.
Giving him the chop.

Violet

When I learn how the violet
lets you breathe its perfume only once
(a single sniff enough to freeze the nose
or nudge a bewildered bee to a neighbouring flower)

I find myself in my grandparents' house —
back in that cold and Sunday-best front-room,
lured by the muffled sounds of derring-do
that steal from the big glass-fronted bookcase.

Hannay, Wimsey and Bulldog Drummond wait
while I open the tiny bottle lying
forgotten in a drawer of the empty desk:
little more than a brownish stain, it breathes

my shy grandmother's name into the air.
Huddled into the armchair's fuzzy plush,
I am the heroine drenched in Parma violets
stepping out on the arm of the Saint

in Paris or New York. And if they come
looking for me, I know they'll pause
in the open doorway, puzzled
by a scent that shimmers

like a halo in the air. But I
am in Chicago, so never hear them
when they turn to call back down the stairs,
"She isn't there!"

Fretwork

(in memory of my grandparents, Vi and Will Kane)

An awkward, gruff *Dockyardy*, your hands thought
for you. Spreading the loaf-end with butter,
cutting each thin slice as though it mattered,
you were the caulker lent to Lilliput.
The fire-screen was your masterpiece: like stout
lace, the Lord's Prayer that your fret-saw stuttered
out; who "never held with church — got better
things to do"; shuffling, when it was wet,

to a resinous bolt-hole off the kitchen, where
you made this glove box I've inherited —
for Vi, who never owned long evening-gloves.
An ark of whittled leaves that lets the air
flow sweetly through. Foolishly grand, fretted
over, mended and handed on, like love.

A Spell in the Screw-Dock

(for Chris and Daphne)

Machinery, like an avenue of palms
on some neglected, rank plantation, hoists
its forty rusting screws skywards. Joists
of greenheart wood connect these paired salaams
with dog-clutch, cogs and gears — our guide warms
to his theme. But I'm distracted by the moist
fragrance of some herb we've crushed — an almost-
yarrow or mayweed whiff of East Neuk farms.
Drying, it's gone — like Heyerdahl's *Ra II*,
last ship to lie here, reeds soon growing buoyant
as months of ocean drained; becalmed by spells
from the island's green heart: rustle — shot through
with grackle-song — of sea-grape, palms, slow chant
of surf. All cancelled by one scent that calls.

Bridgetown, Barbados. April 2000

The Kites of Liquorice Village

(for Colin Hudson)

Waste ground like skin-disease — the running sore
of a sewer, picked bones; scabs of crusted metal
over which Mexican poppies sway their petals
like a laying-on of hands; a tattered
seed-pod like that cage that shamed the harbour,
penning recaptured slaves — runaways, shackled,
pilloried with filth; branded like cattle.
Glendairy's prison shares that reek of failure.
We trudge on past as faceless voices call,
and we wave back. We know it's accident
has set us here, them where they cannot see
the kites of Liquorice Village — swelling sails
in which the caged wind sings, with cross-trees bent
on the Easter-tide, for new worlds, sweet and free.

Bridgetown, Barbados

Homing

Somewhere in the Borders
they start to overtake us: lorries heading south
weaving easily in and out of the fast lane
with their freight — a feather-weight
of racing-pigeons.

As the big transporter hurtles past,
carrying them ever further from home,
imagine each bird —eyes closed,
quiet in the hampered dark —
hearing, above

the slap and whine of canvas,
the siren-song of the power-lines;
the miles unspooling beneath the wheels
into a line of music the mind will tag
with accidentals.

Hills like a drag of darkness,
and that quick tug on the line that says
river; cities and towns like interference,
a twitter of static they'll be released into.
Freed, clocked-out

in ceremonies they patiently endure.
Imagine them soaring then, slipping
a sleeve of air to catch the pull of earth,
attuned to memory's pulse,
to frequencies

of starlight. As they listen in to the firths
with their point and counterpoint —
the lighthouses singing, the bridges — small towns
begin to make sense, and forests breathe out
familiar air.

That clock-face with its tower is known;
that gable-end; this garden drenched with night
and its November smell of bonfires
and creosote, and rain on the sprouts
lighting them home.

Firths and Sounds

Trundling over the Forth to North Queensferry —
Scotrail-and-bridge duet transposing into
oiled pistons — I might be crossing Plymouth
Sound aboard the churning Torpoint ferry;
or bowling over the Tay bridge on the bus
towards Newport, looking west, see
not the rail-bridge, or even the misty girders
of the one that fell, but Isambard Kingdom
Brunel's bridge spanning the Tamar. As though
Tamar, Tavy and Tay were all kin
and, buried in my DNA, there lurked
a gene that carries a love of estuaries:
wide-eyed between-places, where fresh turns salt,
slow with enormous skies; runs tidal, dithery,
laying down shoals or flinging up limpet-shells
and yellow periwinkles among the glasswort
and the buttercups. It took my uncle
months to find our Bakers' graves: baptised
and living in Newquay, Devon, men who rowed
across the Tamar daily to work the forge
in Calstock, Cornwall, where at last they stayed.
Ask me, where do you stay? and I'll say, out,
mid-river, tuned to the pluck of the tide, the lure
of the land; one ear cocked for the sound of the sea.

Revising the Blue Guide to Scotland

(for Michael and Elspeth Wills)

1. Souterrain at Carlungie

At the end of the path — thin and straight
as a parting through thick-braided wheat —
a kissing-gate, then quiet turf.

Curled like a question-mark,
open to the sky, this stony passage
basks like a freshly sloughed skin.

We put it on and wear the stones of August;
feel warm air collude with history
in a buzz of grass-scents; seeing how sun

maintains the annals, and prints
at shoulder-height on old red sandstone
shadow of flower of grass;

common bent, frail, barely
a mouse-mouthful;
recorded now, and again now;

a few *lacunae* while clouds
like small Dark Ages swallow it
or wind queries its importance.

2. *Restenneth Priory*

Only low breathing from a herd
of Charolais on the other side of the palings,
and somewhere, a bean-field in flower.

This is so quiet a place
that a bright piece of glass, fallen
from the extinguished lights of Nectan's church
still rests on stone, catching the sun
in Malcolm's cloister.

Nor is it a butterfly
until the buzzard mews
high on its rounds above Finavon;
patrolling the contours of the hill;
doodling over the vitreous defences.

But then such colour lifts
it stains the air.

3. *Pictish Stone at Aberlemno*

The buzzard circles slowly,
letting us read her under-
plumage like the map
of a place we have forgotten,

then reels herself up
into the sun and vanishes.
Later we follow her spiralings
into stone, and stare

at horsemen crossing a field:
their tuning-fork is pitched
to an unknown key; the mirror
flashes as we drive away.

The 'tuning-fork' and mirror are a common pair of Pictish symbols, thought to
have a dynastic significance, though this is not fully understood.

Mended fence, Barra

after a photograph by John Cooper

Let no smalnesse retard thee; if thou beest not a Cedar to help towards a palace,
if thou beest not Amber, Bezoar nor liquid gold, to restore princes; yet thou art
a shrub to shelter a lambe, or to feed a bird; or a plantane to ease a child's
smart, or a grasse to cure a sick dog.
John Donne, *Essays in Divinity*

Darned like the heel of a sock, like boot-hose,
with baler's twine instead of worsted, with rope
and string and twists of wire, the mended fence
reveals itself as a kind of random knitting.
Purely utilitarian, this link-work
has a beauty that's all pro tem, ad hoc,
with textures suggestive of the wider picture,
differences: a study in tensions where
the braced immutability of the post,
split and splintered, poker-worked
by shadows of staple-ring and hook,
is relished no less than the angled span
of iron rails as flat as swords, pocked
and grizzled, and buttoned by rivets: and if a line
of galvanised steel opens its arms
like a horizon after rain, or if it receives
the downward skewering twist of wire
that feathers the light like a gannet,
it's accidental; and there is still room
for twine and string, each with its proper weight
and implicated strength, to be roped-in.
Nylon twine radiates sun, fraying,
and ends of string are wanton tassels of frizz,
but this small net of knots and hitches, reefs
and grannies, deters the straying lamb and plays
cat's cradle with the wind as it lingers or passes,
muttering (to a droned continuo
of shepherd's thyme and turf and gorse, sheep's dung,
sea-weed, diesel) snatches of things like

if thou beest not a Cedar
and
no man is an island
and
make do and mend.

Parable

(for Miquel Desclot)

Dying at Jarrow, Bede
held up his hand, and blessed
his brothers with all he owned: a length
of linen, incense, a box of pepper.

Go home and spread the cloth;
set bread upon the table, fill
the pepper-mill, a jug of water;

and when you have lit the candles,
see how your cupboards full of things
retreat into the shadows;

as you bite into a peppercorn
and fragrance bursts upon your tongue,
it will come to you in a rush how less
is more, and little much.

The Great Tay Wave

"Was you ever stung by a dead bee?"
Walter Brennan as 'Eddie' in *To Have and Have Not*, Howard Hawks 1944

You can only sit on the sand
cradling your angry foot
from which you've plucked
a barb the size of an eyelash,
feeling the fleshy ball swell up
and a pulse begin to take root
like a red-mouthed flower.

You stare at the bee where it lies
on the tide-line, a fuzzy seed-head
or crumpled badge a child has lost.
And though you can't quite believe
that something so withered, so obviously
long dead, could have delivered
this shot of fire that's stopped you

in your tracks, you vow that never again
will you under-estimate the long arm
of the past — yesterday's betrayals buried
like mines beneath a dance-floor; old wrongs
that sit out the centuries like plague
between a bible's pages, like fleas, snug
in a peddler's bundle; or the blow to the shins

become an embolism sailing slowly
towards a certain day in the lungs.
For witness the Great Tay Wave,
that six-foot wall of water barreling
the fourteen miles from Killin to Kenmore,
November the 3rd 1755: In Lawers
they gaped at it in wonder, not

knowing it for the observable oscillation,
the seiche, that travels in the wake
of a huge quake far-off; still less
for a messenger surfacing two days late
from the smoking ruins of Lisbon: an arm
reaching out of the rubble,
a voice below your feet.

Eve of another war

(for Alison Mitchell)

In Milton of Balmaha,
war creeps closer on mossy feet;
the only sound the Water of Mar
thundering like artillery
on its way to join the Endrick.

I'm cleaning stones, picking at
old badges of lichen. Recording
names and dates, I uncover
deaths from war and childbirth;
epidemics, emigrations.

When moss is scraped away,
you see how *MEMORY* is carved
to make a bower over the name;
D   A   U   G   H   T   E   R
filling the stone from edge to edge.

In quiet kirkyards by Endrick Water
a girl is hovering at my shoulder —
one who crept away from the camp
in Srebrnica while it was dark
to hang herself at the wood's edge.

Pink cardigan catching the morning light,
closed flower among the branches,
she blossomed on to Europe's front-
pages. Unnamed and famous
on our screens at evening.

And when I kneel beside a fallen slab
and peel back a thick rug of grass,
there's a smooth brown underside
like common-or-garden underlay.
A web of roots with mirror-writing.

Words and numerals, raised up
like braille, in paler script,
where earth is searching the stone
with the long, blind fingers of grass
for names, more names.

Underfoot

Strangers strolling here who wonder at
so many crosses set into our streets

learn that these cobbled saltires underfoot
are where men stood and burned with all they thought.

From that appalling smoke the few names
I know are the ones stitched like monograms

into the ground: **PH** who *took above six*
houres to be reduc'd to ashe (the sticks,

like him, were green and full of sap) — a mere
student. And if Pat Hamilton's revered

it's by his peers, who dodge round his initials,
fingers crossed, all mindful of their finals.

GW, dying on that handkerchief
of ground beside the castle, hurled his grief

in Beaton's face — staring down from the window
where they'd hang him.   Over these stones a flow

of feet and hooves and wheels, year after year,
has passed.   But when I see the west on fire,

the sun a molten ball on the horizon,
it's Pavel Craw I think of, toiling to turn

the scriptures into his Czech tongue; honest
alchemy that cost him.   His voice, first.

The Church ordered a brass ball be hammered
into his mouth: stoppered, he wouldn't stammer

out some brazen cant before the flames
had stifled him. Perhaps they hoped his name

would blow away. He has no stone, no mark,
and on the spot the brewers' lorries park

to unload the city's lingua franca. Above
it all, the gulls crying, over and over.

Patrick Hamilton, George Wishart and Pavel Craw were reformers who were
burnt for their beliefs in St Andrews.

The shadow

after *The Balcony Room* by Adolf Menzel, 1845

(in memory of my sister, Rosy, 2.11.1946–21.2.2004)

Since your death,
I've taken to visiting this room.
I like its emptiness, its modest triumphs,
the way sun pours through gauzy curtains
to lay a block of light on the bare floor.
Matter-of-fact. Unheroic. A stillness
big enough to hold a room we shared
as girls, on holiday at Talloires,
releasing a scent of beeswax,
a shimmer of lakewater,
and mountains looming like the future.

The muslin curtains billow
in sprigged folds like a nightdress,
and I picture you, who always dressed with care,
pausing to smooth your skirt
in front of the tall pier-glass.
Within its narrow compass
everything's doubly clear —
the striped sofa, the engraving whose gilt frame
catches the light like a strand of hair.
These two chairs that turn their backs on each other
have ceased a lifetime's conversation.
The sun highlights their uselessness
while touching a curved back
to warmth and colour.

Better to focus on that rough patch
the sun picks out on the opposite wall.
Is it a shadow, occurring as death does,
part of the world outside on the balcony,
or did the decorator simply abandon his task?
I stare at it and take courage from that baldness,
from blemished plaster with a crack at its centre
like the confluence of two rivers; from this faithful
portrayal of things as they really are.

Primula Auricula

(for Jean Johnstone)

Clothed only in blue air,
all of a piece with the sky, and naked
but for the pale nimbus,
the aureole that is your glory —

the way Giotto paints St Francis
relinquishing his inheritance:
waving goodbye to his damask-
and taffeta-gowned family,

the father shimmering with rage.
Giving up samite and paduasoy,
tussore and lutestring, all the baled
stuffs in the halls of the Bernardone:

with only a bit of the Bishop's blue robe
to cover his nakedness,
he'll take the road that sister earth
unrolls like rough grey cloth, unconscious

of the glory Giotto gives him —
the aureole I thought gave you your name.
But it's your modest leaves you're named for:
little ears, like those on brother bear.

Cat and Water

Our thirsty cat is in the bath
lapping the puddle that squats around the plug-hole.
I turn the tap on slowly —
letting out a steady stream
but not enough to startle her.
She drinks and drinks as though she'll never stop.
Then sits up to watch the water.

It falls in a single uninterrupted flow.
A rapier you'd swear was welded metal
from tap to drain.
Or a glassy rope for a glassy snake to climb.
Mysterious, sinister, thin.
The cat replies to her own unspoken question
and probes it with a forepaw.

O now the sword's a shoal of plunging fish
and small-fry jitterbug off shrugged fur.
Again and again
her claws comb and card it like yarn,
unravelling it in twigs and sprays of light.
She frays the rope in a scatter of seeds
or sways it to a whispery rush of sound.

She knows
what we forget.
She knows this stuff's alive.
Dear beautiful prey to be caught and held and let go and
held again.
And when I turn off the tap and she quits the bath
she leaves by way of a blackberry-path of her own.

The French for 'bonfire'

When I asked you to help with weeding,
you dug my cowslips up.
So flower-beds are now off-limits
and you're confined to pruning and burning.
But I can see how much you enjoy
laying about you with that Gurkha knife
our youngest smuggled in from India.
I love to watch you — gentle, cautious
man that you are — hacking at holly
and slashing at rampant beech-hedge
with wild, extravagant gestures;
casting your clothes to the four winds.

Later, the fire absorbs us.
I haul out branches which you feed
into the flames, recoiling
as holly's oils flare, burn green
with little roars of sound that die
in whitish, choking smoke.
We never get through it all.
When it gets dark we call it a day,
gazing, as the fire goes quiet, at depths
of whispering incandescence; molten places;
pulsing, soft-bodied grubs of light
hardening under a feathery crown of ash.

We're hungry. Then it's time for bed.
But even here you're not allowed to rest —
not yet. Your hair still smells of smoke,
and I want your hands to whisper
a tale of blistering encounters,
to tell their hurts and hot abrasions.
My skin is listening.

Sufficient Unto the Day

Bank Holiday Monday. With no fluttery
drop of letters to open the day like a fan,
you console yourself with imagining the postie
having a long lie-in. His heavy bike
is propped up in the shed; his cycle-clips
will dangle from their hook until tomorrow.
He is a babe in the wood his children's voices
make, that cover him like leaves and grasses.

Absolved from all his chores he lies, and smiles
in bliss as mail he doesn't need to shoulder
warms him, as light as eiderdown.
Letters envelope him—airmails, blue
as oceans; down-to-earth, plain buff manilla.
The world's a postage-stamp, where space and time
jostle in patchworked perforations, so Grace
Darling can scull into the Crystal Palace,

or Halley's Comet vote in Europe's third
election, signing an *X* in fireworks;
or Amy Johnson goggle at Ptolemy's map
of Taprobana of 150 AD
(the 1378 version), with *elephas*
maximus ceylonensis. First-day-covers,
Eden's beauties: clouded leopard, fur as
dappled as a shoal of morning cirrus;

and barn owl — Vautor's *lady bright*, haunting
her own madrigal before she ghosts
away — Earth's endangered species. The explorers
come inside to watch TV. Waking,
their father remembers the shining ram's-horn snail,
the shell transparent, empty; ammonite-coils
mapping a barren island; he stretches, yawns,
and hears the garden gather up its silence.

The Palm Magnificat

(for Lal and Priyanka Jayasinghe)

Even under the stun of noon
    she holds persistent parleying
with the wind, hatching and cross-hatching
ways of hindering and spilling sun
    over the green weirs of her leaves.

Her branches mesh and pass in a matching
    of hands or harmless knives,
still glittering with the drops from last night's monsoon-
storm; such slow and patient geometries
    as must beguile the just-arrived

and jet-lagged — gazing in a swoon
    of heat at jalousies-
turned-Jacob's-ladders brushing a heaven too glar-
ing-bright to contemplate — who might surmise
    that in that thresh of light they eaves-

dropped on angelic conversations
    vegetable and benign —
where tireless leaves debate with rooted patience
how they may canopy this house of air,
    these rooms of cool. A roof that's sing-

ular in how its pinions soar
    from dross and wreckage, picked-
over rags, old sacking. Stormbrash, threadbare layers
of tat and débris; leaf-nodes deep in coir
    like Rembrandt's darkest corners; tropic

subfusc of an underbrush
     that's home to murmurous
estates, to seething picnics. Grackle and purple
sunbird perch and dine-out here on lush
     young life, and green parakeet in squalls

     burst on the gloom, then leave. The fruit-
       bats sleep through it all,
waking to quarrel as dusk falls, then glid-
ing off among the fireflies to visit
     the star-fruit in the neighbourhood.

The Pattern of Our Days

Days when we wake to the heron in its tree
we cancel everything,
home in along low, level shafts of light
to the dagger-like beak where it vanishes
under feathered membrane.

Days that take on the pattern of plumage
as other lives brush us, forcing
minuscule shifts; imperceptible, some of them,
as when a campion withers in Spinkie Den
and yet more eider join the pied flock
below the castle; or cheerfully exhibitionist
like the firm of joiners extending their own shed
beside the car-park.

Audible patterns you need to listen hard for.
The one o'clock clicking of snibs
as departmental secretaries hurry away for lunch,
but just detectable through those hymns
played on the bells in the tower,
that drop on the town like rich and gloomy treacle.

Days that coax us on to the parched grass
to eat our lunch and let the wall — that lovely curve
of rosy, mellow brick that we look down on
from your office ordinarily — occlude us.
The once-espaliered pears, too, have broken free
and gone a little wild, making a rampant shade.

Time to bite on a spring-onion
and picture the screen-saver on your Mac
generating its random doodles,
building patterns intricate as snowflakes.
With nobody there to watch, it fills up
every bit of space with coloured pixels

then wipes it clean and starts all over.
Dancing all by itself like the young
dancing-apprentice in the Turveydrops' kitchen,
or even Billy Idol. Leaving us
to imagine the rest of the pattern
and colour it in.

The Bee-Bole Wall

for Netta

It's claimed that pilgrims, ferried across the Forth,
would rest at Riras before they skirted east
round Lahill Crag, north to Lathones, to ford

the Kenly burn and reach Balrymonth. What they
had braved water and weather for — a fistful
of spires lifted out of mist — is yours

for stepping out of doors. The bee-lines of
those patient feet might still be glimpsed from the top
of the tallest tree: the way the tractor writes

its straightest lines across each day, then heads
for home, for what is loved; a voice, singing;
the imagined bee-skep in the bee-bole wall.

Wedding Songs

1. A Loaf of Bread
after Monet's *Haystacks, Snow Effect*

(for Marine and Olivier)

Winter is when you need to see this Monet.
To come in out of the city's filthy streets
and cross his field of snow — crisp as a sheet
or table-cloth — and toast yourself. Mown hay
like those proverbial loaves, to feed the many;
haystacks, round as *pains de campagne*, whose heat
is palpable, might melt the snow; replete
with wordless promises of milk and honey.

This is the bread I wish you for your table.
Food of fiery visions, plain as haystacks.
Giverny in winter may lie shrouded,
silent under snow, with summer's fabled
pond lidded and still, but you'll not lack
for warmth and light and love; for daily bread.

2. Wedding-Dress
after *Vestits de Ceba* — photographs by Toni Vidal

(for Jessy and Andy)

I'm sewing you a dress of onion-skins —
taffeta scraps from Ridley Road; glitter
of gold in Hackney's festival of litter.
Their tawny silk's demotic opulence
suits you: sniff, and you'll breathe a redolence
of Dalston cooking — curry, kebabs and fritters;
back-streets on summer evenings; starling-twitter;
pigeons' soft tête-à-têtes from shady gardens.
Your dress is stitched with these, so, clad with love

you'll go to your guid man.   Remembering
the onion's blessing on us makes us cry,
I've made a dress that's easily removed —
an airy, next-to-nothing, onion-string
of words. You should wear only poetry.

3. A handsel of light

(for Liz and Jamie)

The pale blue cotton ramie of last night —
seersucker, almost, puckered by glancing rain —
transformed by morning into shimmering moiré
a colour somewhere between pearl and grey,
lays itself out in swathe after swathe along the firth;

creased into plissé at the Chanonry,
where Beauly merges into Moray, into
an incomparable dazzle the eye hardly dares
to dwell on: flaws and cross-weave, mended rents
and braidings; rumpled cloth and stubborn slubs

of character made beautiful by light.
As though the sun had borrowed an iron
and set to work to smooth enough silk
for shirts for him, blouses for her,
to last them all their married lives.

Flowerburn Mains, Rosemarkie

Sari

(for Christopher and Daphne)

Four thousand miles from Scotland, we're at home
among the rainy mountains, the fields of leeks
and cabbages, the hills that promise tea.
The train clattered and drummed like the Kandyan
dancers at your wedding, blowing its horn
like the conch that brings the bride to the *Poruwa*.

Those cakes of milky rice you fed each other
swelled and sweetened into days you shared
with us. And now you're hammering at our door
in the *Ella Grand Motel* to tell us that dawn
is the time to see the most amazing view
in the world. *Christopher's waking us up again!*

your father groans — the way you'd prise open
our eyelids, sharing your every moment, or just
a wee boy scared to go for a pee in the dark.
But all your life you've been opening our eyes,
and now you've tiptoed away from your sleeping wife
to coax us over the dew to the edge, to show us

Ella's famous *Gap*: the light is grey
up here in the grassy gods, the wings dark,
but from six thousand feet we can look through
as the play begins, and day unfolds itself
like the sari a man must wrap around his bride.
A sea of rose-gold pearl whose wave-crests

are mountains as far as the horizon; peaks
appearing, sharpening as the bowl fills up
with milk. A hundred miles away, a lake
opens its eye, and though our hanging valley's
dark, the sky is slowly whitening;
a bird tries out its xylophone of notes,

rippling up the octave towards the moment
when a tree in the wings will suddenly glitter,
and colour flood the hill and wash us home
on a tide of waterfalls and spice and sweat
to Colombo, London, Fife; into the world
and all that patterned life we can't yet see.

Lady Prospero

(for Marg on her 60th birthday)

Stepping down off the plane in Gaborone
you declared your books, your tools,
your love of gardening. At your heels
the Ceres burn flowed into Letlhakane,

summoning, Ariel-like, on the very edge
of the Kalahari, guava-trees;
persuading into a bright oasis
cosmos, nasturtiums, Livingstone-daisies; a hedge

of elephant-grass to soar from arid earth.
At night that rustling spelled the trees
of home, weaving the memory
of beech and oak and hawthorn into the breath

of Letlhakane sleeping — Setswana, laughter,
music, a donkey braying like a sad
Caliban, in search of a blade
of grass in a baked land that dreams of water.

Ntwetwe's lake is salt-pan, dazzling, white,
but in Okavango the hippos yawn
like years, and you're thinking you'll cut down
that tree at Viewfield, borrow some African light.

The *go-away* bird's calling fills your sails:
in Ceres, Prospero's rose is needing
pruned, soon you'll be home and weeding,
African dust ingrained, under your nails.

Thistledown

(for Francesc Parcerisas on his 60th birthday)

Do you remember the thistles — *carlines* —
each one pinned like a radiant sunburst
on those thick wooden doors in Farrera?
The sun shone down each day that we were there
so we never saw a single flower earn
its name of *poor-man's-weather-glass*
and close up in a fist, forecasting rain.

This is the time of year when rose-hips
glow like lamps along Farrera's paths,
while here, the thistles are all thistledown
and feasts for goldfinches. And I think
you'd want to know (if you don't already, that is)
that when they flock together they're called a *charm*.
And ours was a charmed circle, surely, at work

in the old schoolhouse; the first of your string of lamps
that shine and go on shining like a bridge
across languages. I send you thanks like thistle-
down, via the four winds and those un-
translatable, in-between, mysterious ones —
llebeig, xaloc, gregal, mestral — sure
that this way they'll arrive, whatever the weather.

The Burning-Bush

(for Lluís Llobet and Cesca Gelabert)

Sun strokes my back as I climb,
but puddles along the path are splintered glass
and earth and rock are one.
A scent of crushed thyme underfoot,
medicinal in thin air.
Another month and only smoke
will show where the village lies —
this web of grey-brown roofs
spun from the squat tower
whose eight sides I counted this morning;
the weather-cock is a fire-bird
with tail streaming gold over the birch-woods.

And the wild briar is a revelation,
a burning-bush
between me and the sun.
All the rose-hips are on fire,
each vermillion fruit a drop
of molten sealing-wax;
enough for a hundred letters,
and promise of more.
With one robin's pincushion — love's
whiskery exemplar — flaw turned
to beauty in the beholder's eye.

I put out a hand
to block the sun's dazzle, but light
squeezes between my fingers, and shows
flesh and bones in a blur of blood.
Suddenly it's cold,
and I turn and follow the sun
down the mountain.

Farrera de Pallars, November 1998

Water-wheel

after an early photograph in the Bestard Archive, Mallorca

Behind the glare of white hotels, inland
where dusty trees stand ringed with fallen fruit —
oranges, lemons in a rickle of light —
you can still find the wells, mute and abandoned,
the wheel that once dipped splashing underground
all smashed, poking through tumbled parapet,
a dead thing with its ribs bleached white by drought.

Now look. Here's the well working, loud with the
    drowned
clatter of wood and thresh of water; simple
machinery the mule can turn blindfold
in plodded hours around the perimeter;
of slower, greener times the innocent symbol,
he stands transfigured, backlit by the field
of almond-blossom spraying up like water.

In the Alfàbia Gardens

Every year there are more villas,
each with its pool
set like a turquoise or aquamarine;

as you drive past the golf-course
with its sprinklers going at noon,
seeing how trees

are shedding their leaves in May,
aware of the water-table
silently dropping,

you keep on harking back
to a spring that never,
even in the hottest summer, fails;

hearing the ghosts of three water-mills
still prattling in the splash
of fountains in Alfàbia's gardens;

vocabulary bundled
in runnels, conduits, cisterns;
gutturals of a banished tongue

that sang through *sènies* and *assuts*
pour clamorous from *alfàbies;*
are stored like memory in stone *aljubs.*

And you remember how their word
for a misshapen pearl
means *drop of water;*

a people who prized
water above gold;
their language cursive,

shaped like the meniscus' curve
over the brimming cup
held out to a stranger.

Walking beneath the palms they planted,
where pool after pool drops down,
you reflect how water everywhere

underwrites everything:
the damask-rose, smelling of mercy,
the pomegranate's globes

packed tight with justice;
the pergola's arabesques of spray,
geometry like an idea of perfection.

And from the *glorieta* you can hear
Alfàbia's perimeters brim over
into fig and almond orchard;

water's acoustic flowing into
pasture for grazing sheep, into
the sweet and constant trickling of their bells.

sènia (Arabic in origin), water-wheel
assut (Arabic in origin), sluice-gate
alfàbia (Arabic in origin), water-jar
aljub (Arabic in origin), water-tank, cistern
glorieta (Catalan), arbour

Moon Into Marmalade

(for Stewart Conn, Anna Aguilar-Amat and Francesc Parcerisas)

Oranges
placed in a pan two nights ago
to soften; frozen globes
glowing through their fur of rime.
Cousins to this moon,
her pallor bathed in orange dayglo;
colour that is shadow
and our own.

Full-moon
fruit, round and bright; each O
opens its mouth, and robes
the kitchen in bitter scent. I dream
that over *Montseny* an orange
ripens among night's leaves and, growing,
sweetens, for the moon knows
her own.

Oranges
are pools of juice, and I'm like you,
fishing; my spoon probes
for pips, while overhead a rim
of silver is moving. In the moon-
hoard I'm dipping, luring the brown
words I borrow only,
do not own.

Scops Owl

Tonight I lie without you
under a pelt of darkness
heavy with cypress
ragged with goat-cries.

Under the white moon's Roman coin
dogs are barking from distant farms
with little rips of sound
that stone walls catch, throw back.

All this he draws like silk
through a gold ring
into a single woodwind note,
tongued and sweet—

a true and level fluting
I picture travelling
through night's horizons
north, to where you sleep.

La Font, Pollença July 2000